SECRETS of NATURE
from
A - Z

DR. TUGLER

Illustrated By Salvador Capuyan.

To order additional copies of this book, contact:
Xlibris
844-714-8691
www.Xlibris.com
Orders@Xlibris.com

ISBN: Softcover   978-1-6698-4400-6
            EBook   978-1-6698-4399-3

Print information available on the last page

Rev. date: 08/24/2022

CONTENTS

Dear parents,

You could read this story with your smart, curious children who are interested in investigation, science, and nature. Teachers could use it in class to read and analyze different situations with the students. This story is for young adults and others, especially those interested in science, solving problems, and investigation.

To all readers: This book could help improve your knowledge of different realms of nature and sharpen your intellectual skills.

In the books you will get acquainted with space pirates and students of Galactic University, smart octopi and even smarter whales, disputing chemists, and oil-miners! These and other book characters will take you to space and underground, to the North Pole and to the African desert, to mountains and waterfalls, to warm snow and cold fire, and even to listen to an echo. All these fantastic adventures are waiting for you in the series.

LET'S START WITH LETTER
A

APPROACHES DIFFER

Communicating vessels are vessels that are connected. If a homogeneous liquid is in them, its level should be the same in both vessels. That is the law!

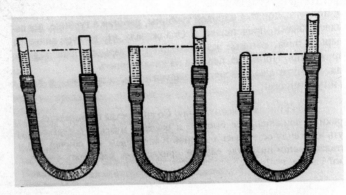

Water: Yesterday I was poured into communicating vessels.

Mercury: Oh, really! I was there yesterday too.

Water: What did you think?

Mercury: It wasn't fun. Some oil was pushing me from the right. You know me –

I didn't yield a millimeter to it. Anyway, it raised its head above mine!

Water: Why did that happen?

Mercury: When two different liquids are in communicating vessels, their heights have an inverse relationship with their densities. The less dense the liquid, the higher it rises. The oil had a low density, and it thought that was a reason to be proud – just because it can always keep its head above mine.

Water: I was in three different communicating vessels yesterday. I was there alone, but the whole time one part of me was higher than the other. Different vessels, different feelings!

Mercury: What do you mean?

Water: I was on different levels in the communicating vessels, while the pressure in them was the same. How could that happen? I was sure that the *law* of communicating vessels cannot be violated!

Mercury: Of course not! We cannot tolerate injustice!

Water: A friend of mine said that the most important thing is the shape of the meniscus, which is a curved surface of liquid in a vessel. The shape in each vessel is different. If it is convex, the pressure under it is greater.

Mercury: And if it is concave?

Water: The pressure under it lessens.

Mercury: Oh, so that's the reason! You know, I was almost ready to sue those vessels for violating the laws.

Water: That's nothing in comparison to what I'm going to tell you now. My sister, Soap Water, was invited to Hollywood to make soap bubbles. You know, they were shooting a "soap opera" there some time ago!

Mercury: The name sounds familiar... So what happened?

Water: It was almost a detective story. When they took a straw and made a soap bubble on each end of it, one of the bubbles was bigger than the other; the small one started to get smaller, the big one - bigger.

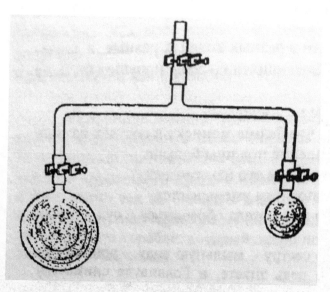

Mercury: Why was that?

Water: That's what I asked my sister. And she said that I don't know physics. Can you believe that? Me! Not know physics!

Mercury: Did you tell her that you have a master's degree?

Water: Yep!

Mercury: I think that the clue to all this is the curved surface of a soap bubble.

Water: What do you think this curve depends on?

Mercury: It depends on the radius of the bubble. The smaller the radius, the greater the curve.

Water: What about the pressure inside the bubble? Do you think it depends on the size of the bubble?

Mercury: Definitely. The greater the curve, the greater the pressure. The small bubble produces greater pressure on the air inside the straw than the big one. That is why the small bubble gets smaller and smaller and finally collapses.

Water: The small always suffer!

Mercury: It has nothing to do with suffering. It is a science called *Physics*.

Water: Physics? Oh yeah, physics! It's a very interesting science. Laws and something else...

Mercury: The collapse of bubbles, or cavitation, as scientists say, seems to be harmless. But sometimes it causes tragedies. A friend of mine, a blade on the wheel of a gas turbine, got covered with hollows. Can you imagine that? These hollows formed because of the gas bubbles. When they collapse, they hurt the blade. Now my friend is on disability, and they don't even care.

Water: Scandalous! It's a violation of all laws!

Water was boiling from indignation! Bubbles were rising from the bottom of its vessel, moving faster and faster towards the surface. Mercury looked cold and shiny as usual. It was trying to remember where else it saw cavitation. It didn't seem to be long ago. But where was it?

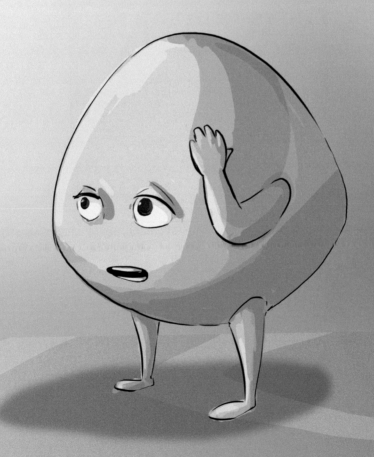

Dear parents,

For your children to understand this story clearly, we prepared investigative questions and answers for them. You could use the answers if you need them to discuss "Approaches Differ" with your children. But first ask them to try to find the answers in the story.

Dear Children! Are you a detective? Find the **a**nswers for the questions in the text.

Questions

1. What are communicating vessels?
2. What is a homogeneous liquid?
3. What is the law of communicating vessels?
4. Why did oil raise its head above mercury?
5. What is the meniscus?
6. What is the shape of a meniscus?
7. How does the meniscus affect the pressure of liquid?
8. Is the phenomenon in #7 a violation of the law of communicating vessels?
9. Why did the characters want to sue?
10. Why was one bubble in the straw bigger than the other one?
11. How does the curve depend on the radius of the bubble?
12. How does the pressure in the bubble depend on the radius?
13. What is Physics?
14. What does the word Physics mean?
15. What is the phenomenon "cavitation"?
16. Why does cavitation cause "tragedies" in technical devices?
17. When do cavitations happen in your teakettle when it's heating? When it boils or when it starts to heat?

Did you find the answers for the questions in the text?

Answers

1. Communicating vessels are vessels that are connected.
2. Homogeneous liquid is liquid that has constant density everywhere.
3. If a certain homogeneous liquid is placed in them, the liquid's level should be the same in both vessels. That is the law!
4. When two different liquids are in communicating vessels, their heights are in inverse relationship with their densities.
5. The meniscus is the curved surface of the liquid in a vessel.
6. It is convex, flat, or concave.
7. If it is concave, the pressure under it lessens. If it is convex, the pressure increases.
8. This phenomenon is not a violation of the law of communicating vessels because you know how to explain it.
9. They thought that the level of liquid in communicating vessels has to be the same and not dependent on the form of the meniscus.
10. The clue to all this is the curved surface of a soap bubble.
11. The bigger the radius, the flatter the curve. The smaller the radius, the greater the curve.
12. The greater the curve, the greater the pressure. The small bubble produces greater pressure on the air inside the straw than inside the big bubble. That is why the small bubble gets smaller and smaller and finally collapses.
13. Physics is a very interesting science. Laws and something else...
14. Nature
15. The collapse of bubbles.
16. The blade on the wheel of a gas turbine got covered with hollows. These hollows formed because of gas bubbles. When those bubbles collapse, they hurt the blade.
17. When a teakettle heats up, bubbles rise from the bottom, moving faster and faster towards the surface and collapse because water is colder on the surface, becoming cavitations.

How many questions did you answer correctly?

Put the answer by yourself!

1. Water –
2. Mercury –
3. Vessel –
4. Homogeneous –
5. Communicating – vessels
6. Density –
7. Oil –
8. Pressure –
9. Meniscus –
10. Convex –
11. Concave –
12. Violating the laws
13. Soap water –
14. Physics –
15. Radius –
16. Collapse –
17. Cavitations –

Dear Readers! Now you know the **law of communicating vessels.**
Stay with us and you will be smarter. We wish you good luck in your investigation of nature's laws in our next story starting with the letter **A**.

ACCELERATION OF GRAVITY

Acceleration, acceleration, acceleration… The older a person becomes, the more the person's life accelerates: running, tripping, falling. And now there is something known as free-fall due to gravity: how is it free, if the fall is still going to happen?

This is what Stephen, a high school student, was thinking about on the way home. When he came home, he decided to ask his very clever robot, Gene.

Stephen: Listen, Gene. Do you know anything about the acceleration of gravity?

Gene: I know everything that mankind knows. The acceleration of gravity is the acceleration that a body gains while free-falling because of the force of gravity.

Stephen: But why is it called that?

Gene: There is Earth – it produces gravity and the force of gravity, so when the body falls freely, it accelerates. Freedom is only freedom when nothing is blocking the body, including air friction. A body only falls because of the force of gravity.

Stephen: You mean that a body must fall in a vacuum, like on the Moon?

Gene: Yes, like on the Moon. Or on Earth, but only without the atmosphere.

Stephen: So according to Newton's second law of motion, acceleration is proportional to force, right? The stronger the force of gravity, the more the acceleration of gravity should occur. However, the acceleration of gravity for all bodies is the same on this planet.

Gene: That is correct. The acceleration of gravity for all bodies is the same on this planet. It only changes if you go to another planet with a different field of gravity. With different mass…

Stephen: How could we allow this controversy? How come any acceleration is directly proportional to force, but the acceleration of gravity isn't dependent on the force of gravity? It's free of the force of gravity.

Gene: The force of gravity is directly proportional to mass. Do you agree? That is why increasing the mass of a body several times calls for the increase of the force of gravity in the same number of times at the same moment. So their relationship stays constant. This constant relationship is equal to the acceleration of gravity.

Stephen: Don't you mean the acceleration of gravity is equal to about 9.8 m/s^2 (9.8 meter per second in a second)?

Gene: That is the acceleration of gravity on Earth. It only changes if the field of gravity changes. Do you want to go to another planet to verify the result?

Stephen: We'll fly to another planet in the future. Thank you for the explanation about the acceleration of gravity.

Gene: No problem. It is what I was created for.

Stephen: Then can I ask another question I'm interested in?

Gene: Sure, I am ready.

Stephen: Why does a string rip? I think that it rips where it's the thinnest. Therefore, a homogeneous piece of string can't be ripped by any force, since there are no thin parts.

Gene: But the experiment shows that it is possible to rip any string.

Stephen: You are, as usual, correct. How could we allow *this* controversy?

Gene: One can find the solution to the deception in this problem if one knows that there is no such thing as equal thickness and homogeneous material.

Stephen: Why is that?

Gene: Because the force of gravity cannot be made the same in all points of tension.

Stephen: Even in the condition of weightlessness?

Gene: Even in the condition of weightlessness, the string will not be homogeneous because of heat fluctuations.

Stephen: Hypothetically, if we somehow created a homogeneous string, what would happen?

Gene: Even if we created a homogeneous string, the rip would still be able to occur: the string would be divided into individual molecules.

Stephen: Don't fantasize. How could it be divided into molecules if there is no weak point?!

Gene: But the force is infinite. So the string would divide into molecules at the same moment.

Stephen: I would never be able to predict that. Even the thought of it is scary: a homogeneous piece of string divides into molecules at the same moment…

Gene: Logic, my friend, is a great thing. And the knowledge of the laws of nature, of course.

Stephen: And yet people still think that robots cannot figure things out logically...

Gene: If I could laugh, I would. My logic depends on the way I was programmed to work. Clearly, I was programmed by a capable person.

Stephen: Gene, people could make mistakes because they are not robots. It's not like there are programs to control peoples' functions.

Gene: But there are programs in people. They are written in peoples' genes.

Stephen: Genes? Are they like you, Gene?

Gene: Completely different. The genes in people are deoxyribonucleic acid (DNA).

Stephen: It's hard to pronounce that...

Gene: It comes from the Greek root genos, which means gender, existence, and hereditary information.

Stephen: That makes more sense.

Gene: A gene contains the hereditary information needed for the formation of a specific characteristic. The gathering of all the genes of the organism forms the organism's genetic make-up, or genotype.

Stephen: Wow, what a fancy phrase...

Gene: I can, of course, explain it in my own words.

Stephen: Yes, please try to.

Gene: When a person is born, the person already has a program. This program is called a gene.

Stephen: Now I get it. A gene makes me look like my parents, grandparents, and other relatives. A person is free to choose his own course of actions, but a robot can only work according to its program.

Gene: Poor robots... If I could cry, I would.

This whole time, Gene was not only talking, but also making lunch, sharpening pencils, doing the taxes, and installing a router. "I can't imagine that all his abilities are in a program installed into him," thought Stephen. "I think that he can think independently with all the programs installed in him. I wish I could be like that." Dear readers, what do you think? Who is right: Stephen or Gene? Who has more logic: man or computer?

Dear parents,

For your children to understand this story clearly, we prepared investigative questions and answers for them. You could use the answers if you need them to discuss "Acceleration of Gravity" with your children. But first ask them to try to find the answers in the story.

Dear Children! Are you a detective? Find the answers for the questions in the text.

Questions

1. What is acceleration of gravity?
2. What is free-falling?
3. Where could you find a vacuum?
4. Is the acceleration of gravity different for various bodies?
5. How do you change the acceleration of gravity?
6. What is the force of gravity?
7. How does it depend on mass?
8. What is the value of acceleration of gravity on Earth?
9. Is it the same on another planet?
10. Why does the string rip?
11. Could we rip a homogeneous string?
12. Why could we rip homogeneous string?
13. What is human programming like?
14. Could a human change his program?

Answers

1. The acceleration of gravity is the acceleration that a body gains while free-falling because of the force of gravity.
2. A body only falls because of the force of gravity.
3. On the Moon or on the Earth, but only without the atmosphere.
4. The acceleration of gravity for all bodies is the same on this planet.
5. It only changes if you go to another planet with a different field of gravity. A planet with a different mass would have a different field of gravity.

6. Earth produces gravity and the force of gravity so when the body falls freely, it accelerates. A body only falls because of the force of gravity. Therefore, increasing the mass of a body several times calls for the increase of the force of gravity in the same amount of times at the same moment. So their relationship stays constant. This constant relationship is equal to the acceleration of gravity.

7. The force of gravity is directly proportional to mass.

8. The acceleration of gravity is equal to about 9.8 m/s² (9.8 meter per second in a second).

9. It only changes if the field of gravity changes when you go to another planet.

10. It rips where it's thinnest. Therefore, a homogeneous piece of string can't be ripped by any force, since there are no thin parts.

11. A homogeneous piece of string can't be ripped, since there are no thin parts. But even in the condition of weightlessness, the string will not be homogeneous because of heat fluctuations.

12. The force of gravity is infinite. So the string would divide into molecules at the same moment.

13. There are programs in people. They are written in genes.

14. A person can't change his genes.

Glossary

1. Acceleration: it is when speed increase
2. Gravity: takes place around each mass
3. Robot: machine
4. Atmosphere: the ocean of air around the Earth
5. Field of gravity: around all masses (bodies)
6. Force: it appears when one body interacts with another
7. Mass: measure of inertia of a body
8. Planet: cold object in the universe
9. Weightlessness: when a body doesn't apply pressure to a surface after freely falling with the acceleration of gravity
10. Molecules: the smallest amount of substance with the same features
11. Density: the amount of mass in a single unit of volume

12. Homogeneous liquid: when density is the same everywhere
13. Logic: if all men can die and Jon is a man, then Jon can die
14. Genus: program of a man

Dear Readers! Now you know the **acceleration of gravity.** Stay with us and you will be smarter. We wish you good luck in your investigation of nature's laws in our final story starting with the letter **A**.

AUTOMATONS

Dear readers, get ready. We are approaching automatons. We don't even need to come any closer. We can hide behind these bushes, and we will be able to see and hear everything. There is a robot and an android right in front of us. They are both automatons. The only difference is that the robot does not look like a human being, while the android is a perfect copy of one. But it is not surprising. The Greek word *android* means *manlike*. We see the robot and the android standing near each other and automatically shuffling from foot to foot. They really want to talk about something, but they don't know how to start a conversation.

Robot: I am starting a conversation now. I am a robot. I am very smart. In a way, I am similar to human beings. Human beings have the ability to think. My actions are so logical that it can be considered that I also think. My ancestors, robots of earlier generations, told me that I will become even smarter, because I learn from people, or as they say, they will upgrade me. They will increase my memory and the speed of my reaction. But even though I learn from humans, I really am smarter than they are. I am not going to tell them that. But I'll tell you. My memory is so vast that people often come to me with complicated questions, and I give them an answer. Obviously, my electronic brain must be improved all the time, to keep me up-to-date.

Android: I am continuing the conversation. I am an android.

Robot: It is a very nice name.

Android: It is not a name.

Robot: Sorry, you are not clear. Aren't you a human being?

Android: I have just said I am an android. I am not a human being, though I deserve to become one. It should be easy... And what about you? You are a robot. You are not a human being either, right?

Robot: Are you asking me what a robot is? The word *robot* comes from a Czech writer, Karel Chapek. More than seventy years ago he wrote a fantasy, *R.U.R.*, or *Rossum's Universal Robots*. In this play, universal workers, robots, looked exactly like human beings and could do any work human beings did. At the same time, they only had a mechanical perception of this world. It did not take too long before robots appeared in scientific articles and technical projects. Robots are machines which do work in place of humans. Is it clear now?

Android: Absolutely. A meat grinder is a robot, because it works instead of human beings. It grinds meat.

Robot: A meat grinder is not a robot.

Android: Hmmm... Maybe a TV set is a robot?

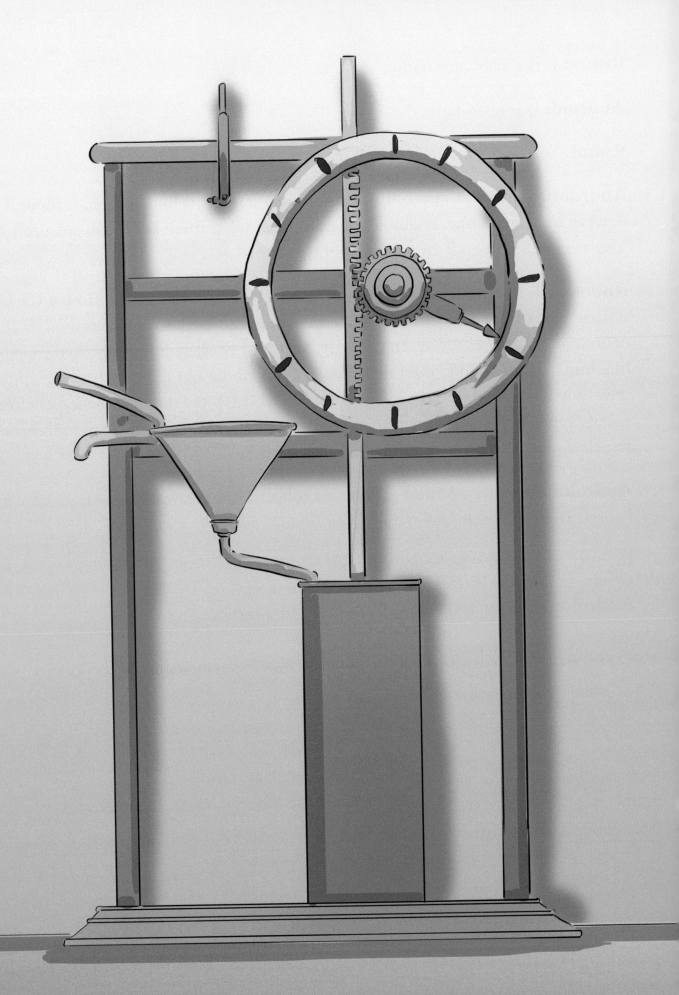

Robot. No.

Android: But why not? What is a robot then? You don't even possess the knowledge, with that vast memory of yours, of what a robot is yourself!

Robot: I know that the first robots are considered to be the machines that had two mechanical arms. Using these arms, they could do some manlike movements.

Android: Big deal! Is that all? Unlike you, I have encyclopedic knowledge of everything about androids.

Robot: Like what?

Android: Long, long ago in ancient China and India they made a clepsydra.

Robot: What did they make? Human beings wouldn't let you use that bad language!

Android: The clepsydra is a water clock.

Robot: Oh, a water clock! OK…

Android: Just imagine a vertical water container. There is a figure of a crying baby at the foot of it. The water from the container goes in the baby's eyes and it looks as if it is crying. All the tears fall to the other container. In that container, a figure of a woman floating on the water surface points to the time scale. As the tears fall, the woman rises, showing the time.

Robot: Fantastic! They are both robots, this woman and the baby. They are my relatives! And the container… This whole clepsydra comprises one robot.

Android: But you do not know your genealogical line! Robots don't look like people. You just told me that you came from mechanical two-armed machines. How can you say now that a clepsydra is your relative?!

Robot: Those are things I can say. Those are my feelings.

Android: Your feelings? What kind of sentence is that? You're a machine! If I had a sense of humor, I would laugh.

Robot: Let's stop arguing about the terminology, my friend. Even in ancient times my relatives were selling holy water in Egyptian temples. These salesperson-automatons were described by the great historian Heron in his books.

Android: That is correct. These selling machines are also robots. And regular mechanical clocks are also robots. They have been in existence for about a thousand years. The first stories about them are dated in the ninth or tenth century. A great Italian scientist, Galileo Galilei, used a pendulum for measuring time. Later, a Dutch scientist, Christiaan Huygens, who worked on improving clocks for many, many years, added a coiled spring that would re-supply the lost energy to the pendulum, so that human beings didn't have to attend to them all the time. Mechanical creations of clock makers were called automatons. Automatons are machines that move or work by themselves.

Robot: Sometimes people give them your name, my friend.

Android: Android is not my name. Androids are just machines that resemble humans because *android* means *manlike*. The best creation of this sort is considered to be the clock presented to the King of Spain, Ferdinand VI in the eighteenth century. A clock is connected to a group of automatons. One of them is an android, a lady sitting on a balcony and reading a book. She seems to be listening to music, which is played by another automaton. And there are two more. One is a small bird which flies up and down and sings. The other is a dog which guards a basket with fruit. If somebody takes something from the basket, the dog barks until it is returned. Another famous android even had a name, *Flutist*. Sitting on a pedestal, he reached about 5'8", around the height of a human being. So he sat on the pedestal and played twelve different melodies on his flute. To make the sounds, he blew the air from his mouth into the flute, while his fingers moved to close the necessary openings on it. Now that's a true android!

Robot: And I have heard that one of the first famous androids was a scribe. He kept writing the same phrase over and over again: "Je ne pense pas, donc je ne suis pas?" Which translated into English is "I do not think, therefore am I not?"

Android: A real human being, a mathematician and philosopher, Rene Descartes, wrote in one of his books, "Je pense, donc je suis" - "I think, therefore I am". Naturally, he had a right to do that. He is a human being! Isn't this in one of your files, my friend, why all these androids - scribes, flutists, musicians - who looked and moved exactly as human beings are not really human beings?

Robot: Why make such a big fuss about human beings? What are they, anyway?

Android: The history of the circus provides us with an answer in the story of Erik Weisz, who lived in the U.S. many years ago. He had another name, Harry Houdini. They even called him *King of Magicians*. Once, in Kansas City, he performed a true miracle for his audience. Imagine! Performing a miracle while hanging upside-down fifteen feet above the earth and wearing a strait jacket! This story holds the answer to your question about the difference between human beings and automatons.

Robot: What do you mean? Tell me more about this Harry Houdini.

Android: Oh, this is a great story. A curious crowd silently watched the tightly swaddled body of the magician rise. Finally, swinging a little, it stopped. Almost right away Houdini's body started to coil, as if it were caught by convulsions. It seemed as if he did not have any bones, because soon the tied-in-a-knot sleeves of his strait jacket were hanging freely below Houdini's head. The magician continued to coil and to spin, and the whole jacket moved down and further down, towards his head. Several more seconds, and the jacket was around Houdini's neck, just like a huge collar. With his free hand Houdini quickly untied all the knots and threw the jacket down. And they say the whole procedure took him just about two and a half minutes. There is no android who can repeat that, and robots are not even worth mentioning. Sorry for being so blunt, my friend.

Robot: I need some time to carefully process this information.

Android: A human being also has several senses that connect him to the world. I am not talking only about the five senses known to everybody: sight, hearing, touch, smell, and taste. A human being also has senses of balance, temperature, hunger, position, movement, atmospheric pressure, and many other very important senses.

Robot: And how do people think? That's what I really want to know!

Android: Are you asking about the techniques of the thinking process?

Robot: Yeah. People believe that they are thinking when they use certain images. But research shows that their minds are working with bioelectrical signals. So it means that people are robots, doesn't it?

Android: But human beings can respond to new information when it's put in front of them. Automatons can only respond to information that has been programmed into them already.

Robot: Maybe we are just missing a chip.

Android: Even so, we are still needed in space, or deep in the oceans, or in environments harmful for humans, like those places with high levels of radioactivity. Sounds comforting, doesn't it?

Robot: Robots can walk exactly as people do. And not only that! We look more and more like people. We even do some things better than they do!

Android: Nobody argues with that. But the creator of cybernetics, Professor Norbert Wiener, once said that the main advantage of a human mind in comparison to a machine is the ability to operate with indistinct notions. While humans can comprehend poems, novels, works of art, and abstract and philosophical ideas, computers will take these things to be something amorphous.

Robot: That is how some humans think that another world exists. I am sure it is not true!

Android: Why not? Human beings create, repair, and turn us on. But who turns human beings on? Could you tell me that?

Robot: There are scientific theories about this. Wow! People say sometimes that we cannot work with indistinct notions! They just do not know anything about us!

Android: But what can we say about them? We still cannot figure out the exact difference between automatons and humans...

Robot: Maybe there is no difference...

The automatons are musing. The question turned out to be too complicated for them. Can people answer it? What do you think, dear readers?

Answer: The difference between human and automatons is that a human being can create automatons and automatons cannot create a human.

Dear parents,

For your children to understand this story clearly, we prepared investigative questions and answers for them. You could use the answers if you need them to discuss "Automatons" with your children. But first ask them to try to find the answers in the story.

Dear Children! Are you a detective? Find the answers for the questions in the text.

Questions

1. What is the difference between a robot and an android?
2. What does the word android mean?
3. What does the word robot mean?
4. What is a clepsydra?
5. What are automatons?
6. What was the King of Spain's present?
7. Who is Harry Houdini?

Answers

1. They are both automatons. The only difference is that the robot does not look like a human being, while the android is a perfect copy of one.
2. The Greek word *android* means *manlike*.
3. The word *robot* comes from a Czech writer, Karel Capek. More than seventy years ago he wrote a fantasy, *R.U.R.,* or *Rossum's Universal Robots*. In this play, universal workers, robots, looked exactly like human beings and could do any work human beings did.
4. The clepsydra is a water clock.
5. A robot and an android are both automatons.
6. The clock presented to the King of Spain, Ferdinand VI in the eighteenth century. The clock is connected to a group of automatons.
7. Harry Houdini's given name was Erik Weisz, who lived in the U.S. many years ago. They called him *King of Magicians*. Once in Kansas City he performed a true miracle for his audience. He performed a miracle while hanging upside-down fifteen feet above the earth and wearing a strait jacket.

1. Upgrade: makes an automaton do things better
2. Genealogical line: family tree
3. Pendulum: an object that periodically oscillates
4. Flute: musical instrument
5. Senses: help a human see, touch, hear, smell, taste, or feel
6. Chip: small piece of electronic equipment that is used in computers and other electronic equipment
7. Radioactivity: emission of radiation
8. Cybernetics: the study of automatic control systems
9. Indistinct notions: abstract ideas
10. Amorphous: undefined or indefinite

Dear Readers! From the previous stories, you know about the **law of communicating vessels,** the **acceleration of gravity**, and various **automatons**. Stay with us and you will be smarter. We wish you good luck in your investigation of nature's laws in the next book called

SECRETS of NATURE
from
B - Z

The ability to speak, to state
one's thoughts clearly, to
prove a point is not innate...
but this ability can be very
important in everyday
conversation and in
winning arguments.
To help you learn how to
argue effectively and answer
your partner's questions
clearly is the aim of this
book. You will find a
variety of dialogues inside
in which different characters
try to prove their point of view
on different subjects basing
their arguments and statements
on the laws of science.

Printed in the United States
by Baker & Taylor Publisher Services